CHEERLEADERS VS UMPIRES

LIVING TRUTHFULLY AND BOLDLY IN CHRIST

Ron Brown

Cheerleaders vs Umpires

ISBN: 978-1-938254-43-7

Cross Training Publishing
www.crosstrainingpublishing.com
(308) 293-3891

TABLE OF
CONTENTS

Ron Brown

VIEW THE VIDEO THE BOOK WAS BASED ON

DISCIPLESHIP STUDIES

Wes Neal's groundbreaking research produced two books for athletes and coaches. Each provides a complete biblical worldview for sports. There's also a video series from Ron Brown that supplements the books at www.kingdomsports.online. The new workbook edition of the Handbook is recommended for discipleship or small-group studies. These studies along with books written by Ron brown can be found at the Cross Training Publishing website.

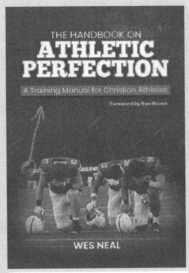

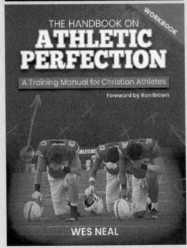

Cross Training Publishing
www.crosstrainingpublishing.com

INTRODUCTION: A CALL TO STAND

A New Creation in a Dark World

We live in a time when the lines between truth and error, right and wrong, are increasingly blurred. In today's culture, which often drifts further from the Word of God, Christians face a profound challenge: will we conform to the shifting standards of the world, or will we stand firm on the unchanging truth of Scripture? The call to follow Christ is not an invitation to blend in but to stand out as shining lights in the midst of darkness. Jesus Himself reminds us, *"Let your light shine before others, so that they may see your good works and give glory to your Father who is in heaven"* (Matthew 5:16). This is not a passive call but an active, bold pursuit of truth and righteousness, no matter the cost.

In this pursuit, we must ask ourselves a fundamental question: Are we cheerleaders or umpires? The cheerleaders' primary role is to support their team, regardless of its performance or how unearned their victory may seem. While cheerleaders can bring energy and enthusiasm, they cannot advocate for what is right when it conflicts with their team's interests. Consequently, even a questionable call by an umpire can be seen as beneficial if it aids their team. Conversely, a favorable call may be viewed unfavorably if it disadvantages their team.

On the other hand, umpires are called to an entirely different standard. Their role is not to favor one side or the other but to uphold truth and fairness according to the rules they've been entrusted to enforce. Umpires are expected to maintain an objective judicial demeanor and officiate a fair game, which means ensuring accuracy and authority in their decisions, regardless of the scoreboard or the approval of fans and teams. Their authority comes from the rulebook. As Christians, we are called to be umpires—people who live by the standard of God's Word, even when it's unpopular or inconvenient.

Paul's words in Romans 12:2 remind us of this calling: *"Do not be conformed to this world, but be transformed by the renewal of your mind, that by testing you may discern what is the will of God, what is good and acceptable and perfect."* This transformation requires us to anchor ourselves in the Bible, the ultimate "rulebook" for life. Without it, we risk becoming like cheerleaders—swayed by emotions, preferences, or societal trends.

Being an umpire for Christ is not easy. It means calling out sin in our own lives and the world around us. It means standing firm in the face of persecution, misunderstanding, and rejection. But this is the life we are called to live—a life of courage, integrity, and unwavering commitment to the truth of God's Word.

The culture around us may shout, "Don't judge!" or "Follow your heart!" But Scripture teaches us to judge righteously (John 7:24) and reminds us that the human heart is deceitful and desperately wicked (Jeremiah 17:9). To live boldly for Christ is to reject the lies of the world and embrace the transformative power of God's truth.

So, are you a cheerleader or an umpire? Will you carry out your role leaning toward a desired outcome, or will you stand firmly on the Word of God? The choice is yours, but only one path leads to a life that glorifies Christ and makes a difference in the world for His kingdom.

ONE - CHEERLEADERS VS UMPIRES

The Difference in Perspective

One of the most critical challenges facing Christians today is navigating how we engage with a world that increasingly rejects objective truth. The temptation to conform, to avoid conflict, and to seek approval from others is strong. In this environment, the question becomes: will we take the role of a cheerleader, blindly rooting for what benefits us and avoiding the hard truths, or will we take the role of an umpire, standing firm on the objective truth of God's Word, regardless of how it is received? The answer to this question shapes how we live as Christians and how effectively we can impact the world for Christ.

The Cheerleader Mentality

In the context of this analogy, cheerleaders symbolize those who prioritize emotions, loyalty to their group, and personal gain above objective truth. Their role is to rally support for their "team" no matter the circumstances, ignoring faults or wrongs as long as it benefits their side. While their enthusiasm and energy can be captivating, cheerleaders often lack the courage to confront difficult realities or take a stand for what is right when it is inconvenient or unpopular.

In spiritual terms, the cheerleader mentality manifests as a Christian who supports only what aligns with their personal opinions, feelings, or desires rather than the truth of God's Word. This attitude may show up in various ways:

- **Avoiding Confrontation:** Cheerleaders shy away from addressing sin in themselves and others because they fear conflict or rejection. They prefer to maintain peace at any cost, even if it compromises biblical truth.

- **Selective Support:** Cheerleaders cheer for their "team"— their social group, political party, denomination, or personal preferences—regardless of whether it aligns with Scripture. They are more concerned with loyalty than righteousness.

- **Emotion Over Principle:** Guided by feelings rather than facts, cheerleaders are easily swayed by popular opinion or trends. Their commitment to truth is conditional, based on what feels good or what earns them approval.

The cheerleader mentality is dangerous because it prioritizes comfort over conviction and loyalty over truth. Jesus warned against this kind of superficial allegiance, saying, *"These people honor me with their lips, but their hearts are far from me"* (Matthew 15:8). True discipleship demands more than cheering from the sidelines; it requires a willingness to confront sin, proclaim truth, and follow Christ, even when it is costly.

The Umpire Mentality

In contrast, the umpire mentality represents a Christian firmly rooted in God's Word and committed to living by its objective truth. Umpires are not swayed by emotions, opinions, or external pressures. Their role is to call balls and strikes based on a fixed standard, no matter how unpopular their decisions may be. This commitment to accuracy and authority makes the umpire a powerful example of what it means to live boldly and truthfully for Christ.

1. **Guided by Objective Standards**
   The umpire's authority comes from their adherence to the rulebook. In the same way, Christians are called to live by every word that proceeds from the mouth of God (Mat-

thew 4:4). God's Word is our ultimate standard—unchanging, reliable, and authoritative. It provides clarity in a world of confusion and is a foundation for making righteous judgments.

2. **Unafraid of Unpopularity**
   An umpire does not make calls based on the crowd's reaction or the players' preferences. Similarly, Christians must stand firm in their convictions, even when it means being misunderstood, criticized, or rejected. Jesus reminded His followers, *"If the world hates you, keep in mind that it hated me first"* (John 15:18). Our commitment to truth must outweigh our desire for acceptance.

3. **Committed to Accuracy and Authority**
   Umpires are trained for years to accurately judge the strike zone. Likewise, Christians must study Scripture diligently to know the truth and apply it faithfully. Paul instructed Timothy, *"Do your best to present yourself to God as one approved, a worker who does not need to be ashamed and who correctly handles the word of truth"* (2 Timothy 2:15). Living as an umpire requires a disciplined and intentional approach to understanding and applying God's Word.

Key Verse: Standing on God's Word

The foundation of the umpire mentality is found in Matthew 4:4: *"Man shall not live by bread alone, but by every word that proceeds from the mouth of God."* Just as physical bread sustains the body, spiritual nourishment from God's Word sustains the soul. The Word of God is not just a guideline; it is the very foundation for life itself. When we root ourselves in Scripture, we gain the wisdom, courage, and clarity to make righteous judgments and live boldly for Christ.

Conclusion: Choose to Be an Umpire

The difference between cheerleaders and umpires ultimately comes down to perspective and priority. Cheerleaders are focused on their own team, their own feelings, and their own comfort. Umpires, however, are focused on truth—objective, unchanging truth that comes from God. As Christians, we are called to be umpires, standing firm on God's Word and calling out truth with accuracy and authority. While the world may pressure us to conform, we must remember that our allegiance is not to the crowd but to Christ. Will you stand boldly as an umpire, living by the truth of God's Word, no matter the cost.

TWO - A BIBLICAL CALL TO TRUTH

Be Rooted in God's Word

In a world filled with shifting values and deceptive philosophies, the call to stand on the unchanging truth of Scripture is more urgent than ever. As Christians, we are not merely called to believe in truth but to know it intimately, live it consistently and proclaim it boldly. This requires deep roots in God's Word, a commitment to study and meditate on it daily, and the courage to reject the cultural lies that often masquerade as wisdom. To live boldly and truthfully for Christ, we must make the Word of God our foundation and guide.

The Importance of Knowing Truth

Just as an umpire spends years learning the strike zone, Christians are called to diligently study and understand God's Word. An umpire's credibility depends on their ability to make accurate and authoritative calls during a game. Similarly, our ability to discern truth from error in our spiritual walk depends on our familiarity with Scripture. Without a solid foundation in the Bible, we risk being misled by the world's philosophies and our own emotions.

One of the greatest dangers Christians face today is biblical illiteracy. Many professing believers are content to rely on secondhand knowledge of Scripture, gleaning only from Sunday sermons or occasional devotions. This surface-level engagement leaves us vulnerable to deception. Paul warns in Colossians 2:8, *"See to it that no one takes you captive through hollow and deceptive philosophy, which depends on human tradition and the elemental spiritual forces of this world rather than on Christ."* Without a deep knowledge of God's Word, we risk being "captives" of the lies of the world.

Illustration: Imagine buying a product that promises incredible benefits, only to find out later that it comes with dangerous side effects hidden in the fine print. You might feel cheated or misled because you didn't take the time to read the details. The same principle applies to Scripture. The Bible contains the "fine print" we need to navigate life wisely. It equips us to recognize and reject deception, offering us clarity and direction in a world filled with confusion.

The psalmist beautifully captures the need to delight in and meditate on God's Word: *"But his delight is in the law of the Lord, and on his law he meditates day and night" (Psalm 1:2)*. A believer rooted in God's Word is like a tree planted by streams of water, flourishing and bearing fruit even in challenging circumstances (Psalm 1:3). To be rooted in truth is not optional for Christians— it is essential for spiritual survival and growth.

Beware of Cultural Lies

The world offers countless messages that sound appealing but contradict the truth of Scripture. These lies are often subtle, disguised as wisdom or empowerment, but they lead us away from

God's design. Let's examine two of the most common cultural lies and the biblical truth that refutes them:

1. **"Follow Your Heart"**

   This message encourages people to trust their feelings and instincts, suggesting that the heart is a reliable guide. However, Scripture paints a very different picture. Jeremiah 17:9 warns us, *"The heart is deceitful above all things and desperately wicked; who can know it?"* Our hearts are not inherently trustworthy; they are influenced by sin and prone to selfish desires. Instead of following our hearts, we are called to follow Christ.

   In John 3:30, John the Baptist powerfully reminds us, "He must increase, but I must decrease." Following Christ means submitting our hearts, desires, and ambitions to Him. It requires humility and a willingness to surrender our own plans for His greater purpose.

2. **"Be True to Yourself"**

   At first glance, this message seems harmless—even noble. But at its core, it prioritizes self over God. The Bible teaches that our primary identity is not found in ourselves but in Christ. Romans 3:23 reminds us, *"For all have sinned and fall short of the glory of God."* Being "true to ourselves" often means embracing our sin nature rather than submitting to God's transformative work in our lives.

   True freedom and purpose are found not in being "true to ourselves" but in being conformed to the image of Christ. As Paul writes in Galatians 2:20, *"I have been crucified with Christ and I no longer live, but Christ lives in me."* The Christian life is not about self-promotion but self-denial, allowing Christ to reign in every aspect of our lives.

A Life Rooted in God's Word

To combat these cultural lies and stand for truth, we must anchor ourselves in God's Word. This requires consistent study, meditation, and application. Consider the words of Jesus in Matthew 4:4: *"Man shall not live by bread alone, but by every word that proceeds from the mouth of God."* Just as we need physical food to survive, we need spiritual nourishment from Scripture to thrive.

1. **Make Bible Study a Priority:** Set aside daily time to read and reflect on God's Word. Start small, if necessary, but be consistent.

2. **Memorize Key Verses:** Equip yourself with Scripture that addresses the cultural lies you encounter. For example, memorize Jeremiah 17:9 to counter the "follow your heart" mentality.

3. **Surround Yourself with Truth:** Join a Bible study, listen to biblically sound sermons, and build relationships with other believers who value truth.

Key Verse: Stand Firm in the Truth

Consider the key verse, Colossians 2:8: *"See to it that no one takes you captive through hollow and deceptive philosophy, which depends on human tradition and the elemental spiritual forces of this world rather than on Christ."*

This verse reminds us why being rooted in God's Word is crucial. Without a firm foundation in Scripture, we risk being deceived by cultural lies and worldly philosophies. Just as an umpire must know the rulebook to make correct calls, Christians must know God's Word to discern truth from deception.

Conclusion

Being rooted in God's Word is not just a recommendation but a command for every believer. Without a solid foundation in Scripture, we are vulnerable to the lies of the enemy and the deception of our own hearts. But when we delight in God's Word and meditate on it day and night, we are equipped to live boldly and truthfully for Christ in a dark and deceptive world. Will you commit to being rooted in truth?

THREE - THE COURAGE TO BE AN UMPIRE

Standing Firm in a Persecuting World

Living for Christ in a world that opposes Him requires courage, conviction, and a commitment to truth. The call to be an umpire—someone who stands firm on the unchanging truth of God's Word—is not easy. It comes with challenges, opposition, and, at times, persecution. Yet, it is the life we are called to as followers of Jesus. We are not here to conform to the world or cheer blindly for our team; we are here to proclaim God's truth, even when it's uncomfortable or unpopular.

Expect Persecution

Standing for Christ means standing against the world's values. This often puts believers at odds with culture, friends, family, and sometimes even other Christians. Paul's words in 2 Timothy 3:12 remind us of this reality: *"All who desire to live godly in Christ Jesus will suffer persecution."* It's not a question of if but when. If we live according to God's Word, the world's opposition is inevitable.

The Christian life is not a cruise ship; it's a battleship. A cruise ship promises comfort, entertainment, and relaxation. Many people approach their faith this way, expecting an easy journey with minimal effort. But Scripture paints a very different picture. We are engaged in a spiritual battle, fighting against the forces of darkness (Ephesians 6:12). This means stepping onto the battle-field armed with God's truth and prepared to face resistance.

Jesus warned His disciples of this truth in John 15:18-19: *"If the world hates you, keep in mind that it hated me first. If you belonged to the world, it would love you as its own. As it is, you do not belong to the world, but I have chosen you out of the world. That is why the world hates you."* Living for Christ will make you stand out, and standing out often invites opposition. But take heart—Jesus has already overcome the world (John 16:33).

Persecution may take many forms—mockery, rejection, exclusion, or even physical harm—but it also serves a purpose. It refines us, strengthens our faith, and draws us closer to Christ. James 1:2-3 reminds us to *"consider it pure joy...whenever you face trials of many kinds, because you know that the testing of your faith produces perseverance."*

Calling Out Sin with Love

Being an umpire means standing for truth, but how we do so matters. Calling out sin doesn't mean being judgmental, harsh, or self-righteous. It means being a loving truth-teller who seeks repentance and restoration.

In John 7:24, Jesus instructed, "Do not judge by appearances, but judge with right judgment." This is a call to righteous judgment rooted in love and humility. Our goal is not to tear others down but to lead them to the transformative power of Christ.

Consider the key verse, Proverbs 27:6: *"Faithful are the wounds of a friend, but the kisses of an enemy are deceitful."* True love sometimes means having hard conversations. Just as a doctor must deliver difficult news to bring healing, Christians must address sin to point others toward repentance and restoration. Ignoring sin may feel more comfortable, but it ultimately harms both the individual and the body of Christ.

However, we must approach these conversations with grace. Ephesians 4:15 instructs us to speak the truth in love. This means:

- **Praying First**: Seek God's wisdom and timing before addressing someone's sin.
- **Checking Your Motives**: Ensure you are motivated by love and a desire to see the other person restored, not by pride or self-righteousness.
- **Using Scripture as Your Guide:** Base your correction on God's Word, not personal opinions or preferences.

Jesus is the ultimate example of calling out sin with love. When He confronted the woman caught in adultery (John 8:1-11), He didn't condemn her, but neither did He excuse her sin. He lovingly told her, *"Go and sin no more."* This balance of grace and truth should guide our interactions as well.

Key Verse: Standing in Love and Truth

Proverbs 27:6 captures the heart of the umpire's courage: "Faithful are the wounds of a friend, but the kisses of an enemy are deceitful." Faithful wounds come from a place of love, even when they hurt in the moment. The world, by contrast, often offers deceitful kisses—empty affirmations that avoid truth and lead to destruction. As umpires, we are called to deliver faithful wounds when necessary, trusting that God's truth is ultimately for the good of those we confront.

Conclusion: Courage to Stand Firm

Standing firm as an umpire in a persecuting world takes courage. It means expecting opposition and embracing the discomfort of addressing sin—not out of judgment, but out of love. The world may reject you for speaking truth, but Christ has already accepted you.

Take heart in Jesus' words from Matthew 5:10-12: *"Blessed are those who are persecuted because of righteousness, for theirs is the kingdom of heaven. Blessed are you when people insult you, persecute you and falsely say all kinds of evil against you because of me. Rejoice and be glad, because great is your reward in heaven."*

Be bold. Stand firm. Speak truth in love. For in doing so, you glorify God and reflect the courage and grace of Christ.

FOUR - ANCHORED IN SCRIPTURE

Practical Ways to Stay Rooted

In a world filled with distractions, lies, and challenges to our faith, staying anchored in Scripture is essential for every believer. God's Word is not just a guide—it's the very foundation of a fruitful Christian life. Psalm 119:105 reminds us, *"Your word is a lamp to my feet and a light to my path."* It illuminates our journey, helps us navigate life's challenges, and keeps us grounded in truth. But staying rooted in Scripture requires intentional effort. It's not something that happens passively or by accident. Here are two practical ways to anchor yourself in God's Word and grow spiritually.

Develop Hunger for God's Word

Just as our physical hunger grows when we regularly eat nourishing food, spiritual hunger grows when we consistently "feast" on Scripture. Many Christians struggle with reading the Bible because they lack an appetite for it. The truth is that regular exposure and engagement cultivate hunger for God's Word. The more time you spend in Scripture, the more you desire it.

Psalm 119:11 highlights the importance of treasuring God's Word in our hearts: *"I have hidden your word in my heart that I might not sin against you."* Making Scripture a priority not only draws us closer to God but also helps us resist temptation, discern truth from lies, and grow in wisdom.

Start Small, Stay Consistent

If you're struggling to establish a routine, start small. Don't aim for an hour of Bible study right away if that feels overwhelming. Instead, begin with just five minutes a day. Read a short passage, reflect on it, and pray over what you've read. Over time, you'll find that five minutes turns into ten, then fifteen, and eventually a deep hunger for more of God's Word.

Application Tip:

- Choose a specific time each day to read the Bible. Consistency is key, whether first thing in the morning, during a lunch break, or before bed.
- Use tools like Bible reading plans, devotionals, or apps to stay on track.
- Start with Psalms, Proverbs, or one of the Gospels if you are unsure where to begin.

Make Scripture a Part of Your Daily Life

Meditating on God's Word goes beyond reading—it involves reflecting, memorizing, and applying it. Think about how you can incorporate Scripture into your everyday activities. Post a verse on your mirror, keep a Bible app on your phone, or set reminders to pause and meditate on a specific passage throughout the day.

The more you integrate Scripture into your routine, the more it becomes a natural and life-giving part of your day. And as you *taste and see that the Lord is good"* (Psalm 34:8), your hunger for His Word will grow.

Surround Yourself with Truth and Accountability

No one can thrive spiritually in isolation. God designed us to grow in community, surrounded by others who encourage us, challenge us, and hold us accountable. Proverbs 27:17 says, *"As iron sharpens iron, so one person sharpens another."* Being anchored in Scripture is not just about personal study; it's also about surrounding yourself with others who value and live by God's Word.

Join a Community That Values Scripture

Find a church, Bible study, or small group where Scripture is central. Being part of a community that prioritizes God's Word helps you stay rooted in truth. These groups provide opportunities for learning, discussion, and encouragement. They also remind you that you're not alone in your walk with Christ.

Be Accountable and Disciple Others

Accountability is essential for spiritual growth. Share your Bible reading goals with a trusted friend or mentor who can encourage you and check in on your progress. Similarly, seek opportunities to disciple others. Teaching someone else about God's Word not only blesses them but also deepens your own understanding.

Application Tip:
- Attend weekly Bible studies or prayer meetings.

- Find a mentor or accountability partner to help you stay consistent in your spiritual disciplines.
- Look for opportunities to mentor or disciple younger Christians, whether formally or informally.

Encourage One Another

Life is full of challenges, and even the most committed believers can feel discouraged at times. Surrounding yourself with truth-filled people who speak life and encourage you in your walk with Christ is vital. Hebrews 10:24-25 reminds us, *"And let us consider how we may spur one another on toward love and good deeds, not giving up meeting together, as some are in the habit of doing, but encouraging one another—and all the more as you see the Day approaching."*

Key Verse: Rooted in God's Word

Consider the key verse, Psalm 119:105: *"Your word is a lamp to my feet and a light to my path."* Without God's Word, we stumble in darkness, vulnerable to confusion and deception. But Scripture illuminates our path, providing clarity, wisdom, and direction. Just as a traveler depends on a lamp to navigate rough terrain at night, believers must depend on the Bible to guide their steps and shape their decisions. Staying rooted in Scripture is not just beneficial—it is essential for living a life that honors God.

Conclusion: Staying Anchored in Scripture

Anchoring yourself in Scripture requires effort, discipline, and community. By developing a hunger for God's Word and surrounding yourself with truth and accountability, you will grow stronger in your faith and more grounded in truth. Remember, staying rooted in Scripture isn't just about knowledge—it's about transformation. As you read, meditate, and apply God's

Word, your life will begin to reflect His character, and you will be equipped to stand firm in a world that desperately needs His truth.

Will you commit to staying anchored in God's Word, not just today, but every day? Start small, stay consistent, and surround yourself with a community that sharpens and encourages you. The rewards of staying rooted in Scripture are eternal.

FIVE - REJECTING THE WORLD'S LIES

Living as a Conduit of Christ

The world is filled with lies that sound appealing but ultimately lead to destruction. These messages—cloaked in phrases like "follow your heart" or "be true to yourself"—may appear harmless, even empowering, but they contradict the truth of God's Word. As Christians, we are not called to live according to the world's standards but to reject its lies and live as conduits of Christ. This means reflecting His character, His truth, and His love in everything we do.

Be the Best Version of Christ, Not Yourself

One of the most pervasive lies in today's culture is the idea that we should strive to "be the best version of ourselves." While this message encourages self-improvement, its focus is on self-promotion, self-esteem, and self-reliance. Scripture, however, calls us to a completely different standard: denying ourselves and becoming more like Christ.

Jesus makes this clear in Matthew 16:24 when He says, *"If anyone would come after me, let him deny himself and take up his cross and follow me."* The Christian life is not about building up our ego or enhancing our personal brand; it is about surrendering to God's will and allowing Him to transform us into the image of His Son. Our goal is not self-glorification but Christ-likeness.

Illustration:

Consider the role of an umpire. An umpire doesn't make calls based on personal opinions or feelings; they submit entirely to the authority of the Commissioner's handbook. Their job is to apply the rulebook accurately and consistently, regardless of how the players, coaches, or fans feel about their decisions. In the same way, Christians are called to submit to God's authority and live according to His Word. Our lives should reflect His truth, not our preferences or desires.

John the Baptist captures this beautifully when he says, "He must increase, but I must decrease" (John 3:30). True growth in Christ begins when we step aside, allowing Him to take center stage. It is only by decreasing our reliance on self and increasing our reliance on Christ that we can truly live as conduits of His grace and truth.

Hate Sin, Love Truth

Another essential aspect of rejecting the world's lies is learning to hate sin while loving truth. The Bible is clear: God calls us to hate sin, not people. Psalm 119:113 says, *"I hate vain thoughts, but your law do I love."* This verse underscores a key principle: we are to despise anything that contradicts God's Word while delighting in His truth.

Addressing Sin in Our Lives

Hating sin begins with examining our own hearts. Before we can address sin in the world, we must confront it in ourselves. Jesus cautioned against hypocrisy when He said, *"First take the plank*

out of your own eye, and then you will see clearly to remove the
speck from your brother's eye" (Matthew 7:5). This doesn't mean
ignoring sin in others, but it does mean approaching correction
with humility and self-awareness.

Loving Truth Enough to Speak It

Loving truth requires courage, especially in a culture that often
rejects absolute standards. When we speak out against sin, it's
not because we are judgmental or self-righteous but because we
care deeply about others and want to see them reconciled to God.
Proverbs 27:6 reminds us, "Faithful are the wounds of a friend,
but the kisses of an enemy are deceitful." True love sometimes
requires having difficult conversations, pointing others to God's
truth, and doing so with grace and compassion.

Rejecting the World's Lies About Love

The world often equates love with tolerance, suggesting that af-
firming someone's choices—regardless of whether they align with
God's Word—is the most loving thing to do. But true love doesn't
ignore sin; it confronts it with the hope of restoration. Consider
how Jesus interacted with the woman caught in adultery (John
8:1-11). He didn't condemn her, but neither did He excuse her
sin. Instead, He said, "Go and sin no more." This balance of grace
and truth is the model we are called to follow.

Key Verse: Loving Truth More Than Comfort

John 3:30, "I must decrease, and He must increase," is a powerful
reminder of our calling. To reject the world's lies, we must allow
Christ to take the throne of our hearts, displacing our own desires, ambitions, and pride. This means loving God's truth more
than our comfort, popularity, or personal opinions. It also means

hating the sin that separates us from God and embracing the truth that sets us free (John 8:32).

Conclusion: Living as a Conduit of Christ

Rejecting the world's lies is not easy, but it is essential for anyone who desires to live as a conduit of Christ. This requires shifting our focus from self-promotion to Christ-likeness, learning to hate sin while loving truth, and boldly standing for God's Word in a culture that often opposes it.

As you go about your daily life, ask yourself: Am I striving to reflect Christ, or am I pursuing the world's standards of success and self-worth? Am I willing to confront sin with love, even when it's difficult?

Living as a conduit of Christ means surrendering completely to His will, allowing Him to work through you to shine His light in a dark world. When we decrease, He increases, and His truth flows through us to touch the lives of others. That is the essence of rejecting the world's lies and living for His glory.

SIX - LIVING COURAGEOUSLY IN CHRIST

Victory Over Fear

Living courageously in Christ is not about being fearless by nature or having a bold personality. True courage is born out of a deep, abiding relationship with Jesus and an understanding of His love for you. It's about stepping into the challenges of life with confidence, not in your own strength, but in the strength of Christ. This kind of courage enables you to live boldly, reject fear, and pursue God's eternal purposes over the fleeting applause of the world.

Courage Rooted in Love

Many people think courage is about hyping yourself up, being naturally brave, or pretending fear doesn't exist. But real courage, the kind that sustains you through trials and spiritual battles, comes from knowing Christ's love for you. The apostle John reminds us in 1 John 4:18, *"There is no fear in love, but perfect love casts out fear."* When you truly grasp the depth of God's love, fear loses its grip on you.

Why? Because fear thrives on insecurity and uncertainty. But when you know that the Creator of the universe loves you unconditionally, has a purpose for your life, and is in control of all things, there's no room for fear to take root. You can face challenges, rejection, and even persecution, knowing that nothing can separate you from the love of God in Christ Jesus (Romans 8:38-39).

The Example of Christ's Love

Jesus is the ultimate example of courage rooted in love. His love for the Father and for humanity drove Him to the cross, where He willingly suffered and died to redeem us. He didn't act out of fear of man or concern for His reputation. Instead, He faced the ultimate trial with courage, grounded in His mission to glorify the Father and save His people.

In the same way, our courage should be fueled by our love for God and our desire to fulfill His purposes. When we act out of love—love for God and love for others—we find the strength to overcome fear and do what's right, even when it's difficult or unpopular.

Practical Application: How to Root Your Courage in Love

- **Meditate on God's Love:** Spend time in Scripture reflecting on passages that remind you of God's love, such as John 3:16, Romans 5:8, and Ephesians 3:17-19.
- **Pray for Boldness:** Ask God to help you act out of love, not fear, in your daily interactions and decisions.
- **Act in Faith:** Take small steps of obedience, trusting that God's love will sustain you. As you step out in faith, your courage will grow.

Live for Eternal Rewards

The world constantly pressures us to seek greatness for ourselves. We're told to pursue success, fame, and recognition. But Scripture calls us to a higher purpose: to live for God's glory and seek His eternal rewards.

Jeremiah 45:5 is a sobering reminder of this truth: *"Do you seek great things for yourself? Do not seek them."* This verse challenges us to examine our motives. Are we striving to build our own kingdom, or are we focused on building God's? Are we chasing temporary accolades, or are we storing up treasures in heaven?

The Temporary vs. The Eternal

The world's rewards—fame, fortune, and applause—are fleeting. They may bring momentary satisfaction, but they can never satisfy the deepest longings of your heart. In contrast, God's rewards are eternal. When we live to glorify Him, we are investing in something that will last forever.

Jesus reminds us of this in Matthew 6:19-21: *"Do not store up for yourselves treasures on earth, where moths and vermin destroy, and where thieves break in and steal. But store up for yourselves treasures in heaven... For where your treasure is, there your heart will be also."*

Living for eternal rewards means shifting your focus from what the world values to what God values. It means prioritizing obedience, faithfulness, and love over personal gain. It also means being willing to sacrifice comfort and convenience for the sake of the gospel.

Practical Application: How to Live for Eternal Rewards

- **Shift Your Perspective:** Remind yourself daily that this world is not your home. Keep your eyes fixed on eternity (Colossians 3:2).
- **Serve Others:** True greatness in God's kingdom comes from serving, not being served (Mark 10:43-45). Look for ways to bless others and share Christ's love.
- **Invest in God's Kingdom:** Use your time, talents, and resources to further God's purposes. Whether it's through giving, volunteering, or sharing the gospel, prioritize what has eternal significance.

Victory Over Fear Through Christ

Living courageously in Christ requires two key shifts: rooting your courage in His love and living for His eternal purposes. When you focus on God's love and His glory, fear begins to lose its power. You stop worrying about what others think or what the world can take from you, and instead, you gain the boldness to live for something greater than yourself.

The apostle Paul modeled this kind of courage in his life and ministry. In Galatians 2:20, he wrote, *"I have been crucified with Christ. It is no longer I who live, but Christ who lives in me. And the life I now live in the flesh I live by faith in the Son of God, who loved me and gave himself for me."* Paul wasn't concerned with earthly success or recognition. His focus was on glorifying Christ and fulfilling his God-given mission.

Key Verse: Courage to Stand Firm

Consider the key verse, 1 Corinthians 16:13-14: *"Be on your guard; stand firm in the faith; be courageous; be strong. Do everything in love."*

The Christian life requires vigilance, strength, and courage. The world will challenge and resist those who stand for Christ, but we are called to remain steadfast in truth. However, boldness without love can become harsh and divisive. True courage is rooted in love—love for God, love for truth, and love for others. We are not called to fight for our own glory but to stand firm for His.

Conclusion: Courage to Live Boldly for Christ

The world will always try to instill fear in you, but God calls you to live courageously. Root your courage in His perfect love, and let that love empower you to face whatever comes your way. Reject the temptation to seek greatness for yourself, and instead, live for the glory of God and the eternal rewards He promises.

True courage is not about being fearless but about trusting God's love and His promises. When you live courageously in Christ, you can face any challenge with confidence, knowing that your life is secure in Him and that your efforts for His kingdom have eternal value. So, step out in faith, live boldly, and let His love and truth guide you every step of the way.

SEVEN - BREAKING THE HUDDLE

Putting Faith into Action

Faith that isn't put into action is incomplete. Many Christians spend their time in the "huddle," gathering for Bible studies, sermons, and fellowship. While these practices are essential, they are only the starting point. The huddle is where you prepare, strategize, and encourage one another, but the real work of the Christian life happens when you step out and live your faith in the world. It's time to break the huddle, get on the field, and play the game.

Don't Stay in the Huddle

Imagine a football team that never leaves the huddle. They might have the best strategy, the most talented players, and a passionate coach, but if they don't break the huddle and run the plays, they will never win the game. This is how many Christians live their spiritual lives. They attend church, participate in small groups, and soak in sermons, but they never step out to apply what they've learned. They remain in the safety of the huddle, avoiding the challenges and opportunities of living out their faith in the real world.

James 1:22 challenges us with this truth: *"Be doers of the word, and not hearers only, deceiving yourselves."* Hearing God's Word is important, but it's not enough. If we fail to act on what we've heard, we deceive ourselves into thinking we are living faithfully. True faith requires obedience and action.

Jesus emphasized this point in the parable of the wise and foolish builders (Matthew 7:24-27). The wise man built his house on the rock by hearing and doing God's Word, while the foolish man built his house on the sand by hearing but not applying it. Both heard the same teachings, but only one put them into practice. Breaking the huddle means stepping out of the comfort of hearing and into the challenge of doing.

Faith in Action: The Real Game

The "real game" of the Christian life happens outside of the church walls. It happens in your workplace, your school, your neighborhood, and your home. It's in these places that your faith is tested and displayed. When you live out your faith, you become a light in the darkness (Matthew 5:14-16) and an ambassador for Christ (2 Corinthians 5:20).

Where the Game is Played

- **At Work or School:** Your integrity, kindness, and work ethic are opportunities to reflect Christ. Do you work as if for the Lord (Colossians 3:23)? Do you treat others with respect, even when it's difficult?
- **In Your Relationships:** Are you quick to forgive, slow to anger, and rich in love? Do your words build others up, or do they tear them down (Ephesians 4:29)?
- **In Your Community:** Are you meeting the needs of those around you? Do you share the gospel with boldness and compassion?
- These are the arenas where your faith comes to life. Breaking the huddle means recognizing that the Christian life is not about staying comfortable—it's about stepping into the messy, challenging, and rewarding work of following Christ in the world.

Practical Steps to Break the Huddle

1. **Commit to Obedience**
    Decide today that you will not only hear God's Word but also do it. This requires intentionality and a willingness to step out of your comfort zone. Pray for courage and clarity to follow where God leads.

2. **Look for Opportunities to Serve**
    Faith in action often means serving others. This could be as simple as helping a neighbor in need, volunteering at a local ministry, or mentoring someone younger in their faith. Service is a tangible way to live out the gospel.

3. **Share the Gospel Boldly**
    Breaking the huddle means taking the gospel beyond your church community. Look for opportunities to share the hope of Christ with friends, coworkers, and even strangers. Remember, it's not about having perfect words but about pointing people to the One who transforms lives.

4. **Face Challenges with Faith**
    Life outside the huddle will include opposition and difficulty. But it's in these moments that your faith grows. Lean on God's strength, remembering His promise in Joshua 1:9: *"Be strong and courageous. Do not be afraid; do not be discouraged, for the Lord your God will be with you wherever you go."*

Key Verse: Be Doers, Not Just Hearers

James 1:22 is a powerful reminder of the importance of breaking the huddle: *"Be doers of the word, and not hearers only, deceiving yourselves."* When we only listen to God's Word without putting it into practice, we miss the point of our faith. Obedience is the natural response to a heart transformed by the gospel.

Consider this: what good is it to know the playbook if you never step onto the field? The Bible isn't just a book of good ideas—it's a manual for living a Christ-centered life. By putting it into action, you demonstrate your love for God and your commitment to His mission.

Conclusion: The Time to Act is Now

It's time to stop staying in the huddle. While Bible studies, sermons, and fellowship are essential for spiritual growth, they are meant to equip and prepare you for the real game of living out your faith. Breaking the huddle requires courage, boldness, and a willingness to face challenges head-on.

As you go forward, remember that the Christian life is not about playing it safe. It's about stepping out in faith, relying on God's strength, and making an eternal impact in the world around you. The game is waiting—will you break the huddle and step onto the field?

IN SUMMARY: BE AN UMPIRE FOR CHRIST

As you reflect on the truths shared in this booklet, one thing becomes clear: the Christian life is not about playing it safe. It's not about standing on the sidelines or blending in with the world's values. The world tempts us to conform, to avoid conflict, and to seek comfort. But as followers of Christ, we are called to something far greater. We are called to stand as umpires who courageously declare the truth of God's Word, even when it's uncomfortable or unpopular.

The cheerleader mentality—the desire to avoid confrontation and prioritize self-interest—may feel easier, but it leads to spiritual complacency. Christ has called us higher. He has called us to take up our cross daily, live out His truth boldly, and shine as lights in a dark and broken world. This is not a path of comfort but a path of purpose. It is the life of those who know their identity in Christ and walk confidently in His love and truth.

Reject the Comfort of Cheerleading

The world will always pressure you to go along with the crowd, to keep silent when truth needs to be spoken, and to prioritize ease over obedience. But as believers, we are called to resist this temptation. Jesus said in Matthew 7:14, *"For the gate is narrow and the way is hard that leads to life, and those who find it are few."* Living courageously for Christ means choosing the narrow path, the one that requires faith, sacrifice, and a willingness to stand firm on the unchanging truth of God's Word.

Like umpires who call balls and strikes with accuracy and authority, we are tasked with declaring what is right and wrong according to the ultimate standard—Scripture. This responsibility is not always easy, but it is always necessary. The world doesn't need more cheerleaders who blindly support what is convenient or popular. It needs umpires who love enough to speak the truth, even when it's hard, and who trust God to work through their obedience.

Remember Your Identity in Christ

The strength to stand as an umpire comes not from yourself but from your identity in Christ. You are chosen by God, redeemed by the blood of Jesus, and empowered by the Holy Spirit. This identity gives you the courage to live boldly, the wisdom to discern truth, and the confidence to face opposition without fear.

Ephesians 1:4-5 reminds us of this incredible truth: *"For He chose us in Him before the creation of the world to be holy and blameless in His sight. In love, He predestined us for adoption to sonship through Jesus Christ."* You are not an afterthought; you are God's beloved, called to reflect His character and His truth to the world.

This identity sets you apart. You are not called to blend in but to stand out. You are not called to live for the approval of man but for the glory of God. Trust in His Word, and let it guide your every step. Remember that you are an ambassador for Christ (2 Corinthians 5:20), representing His kingdom in a world that desperately needs His light and hope.

Final Charge: Live Courageously

As you leave the safety of the huddle and step onto the field, remember the promise of Romans 8:31: "If God is for us, who can be against us?" No matter the challenges you face, you can have confidence that the God who called you is the God who equips and sustains you. His power is greater than any opposition, and His love is greater than any fear.

So, reject the comfort of cheerleading. Stand firm as an umpire of God's truth. Trust in your identity as a chosen, redeemed, and empowered child of God. Live boldly, love deeply, and let every step you take be guided by His Word. The world may be dark, but you are a light. The field may be difficult, but you are not alone. And the victory, ultimately, belongs to Christ.

Go forward with courage, knowing that your life, lived faithfully, has eternal significance. The world may resist you, but God is with you, and His truth will always prevail.

more than Winning

discovering GOD'S PLAN FOR YOUR LIFE

In most athletic contests, a coach prepares a game plan ahead of time. God designed a plan for our lives before the world began.

God is holy and perfect. He created us to love Him, glorify Him, and enjoy Him forever.

WHAT IS GOD'S STANDARD?

The Bible, God's playbook, says that the standard for being on His team is to:

Be holy.
"Be holy, because I am holy." - I Peter 1:16b

Be perfect.
"Be perfect, therefore, as your heavenly Father is perfect." - Matthew 5:48

WHAT IS GOD'S PLAN?

God created us to:

Love Him.
"Jesus replied: 'Love the Lord your God with all your heart and with all your soul and with all your mind.' " - Matthew 22:37

Glorify (honor) Him.
"You are worthy, our Lord and God, to receive glory and honor and power, for you created all things, and by your will they were created and have their being." - Revelation 4:11

Enjoy Him forever.
Jesus said, "...I have come that they may have life, and have it to the full." - John 10:10b

Why is it we cannot live up to God's standard of holiness and perfection? Because of...

Man's Problem

Man is sinful and separated from God.

WHAT IS SIN?

Sin means missing the mark, falling short of God's standard. It is not only doing wrong and failing to do what God wants (lying, gossip, losing our temper, lustful thoughts, etc.), it is also an attitude of ignoring or rejecting God, which is a result of our sinful nature.

"Surely I was sinful at birth, sinful from the time my mother conceived me." - Psalm 51:5

WHO HAS SINNED?

"For all have sinned and fall short of the glory of God." - Romans 3:23

WHAT ARE THE RESULTS OF SIN?

Separation from God.
"But your iniquities [sins] have separated you from your God..." - Isaiah 59:2a
Death.
"For the wages of sin is death..." - Romans 6:23
Judgment.
"Just as man is destined to die once, and after that to face judgment..." - Hebrews 9:27

This illustration shows that God is holy and we are sinful and separated from Him. Man continually tries to reach God through his own efforts (being good, religious activities, philosophy, etc.) but, while these can be good things, they all fall short of God's standard.
"...all our righteous acts [good works] are like filthy rags." - Isaiah 64:6b

There is only one way to bridge this gap between God and man. We need...

God's Substitute

God provided the only way to be on His team by sending His Son, Jesus Christ, as the holy and perfect substitute to die in our place.

WHO IS JESUS CHRIST?

He is God.
Jesus said, "I and the Father are one." - John 10:30

He is Man.
"...the Word (Jesus) was God...The Word became flesh and made his dwelling among us." - John 1:1,14a

WHAT HAS JESUS DONE?

He died as our substitute.
"...God demonstrates his own love for us in this: While we were still sinners, Christ died for us." - Romans 5:8

He rose from the dead.
"...Christ died for our sins...he was buried...he was raised on the third day according to the Scriptures, and ...he appeared to Peter, and then to the Twelve. After that, he appeared to more than five hundred..." - 1 Corinthians 15:3-6

He is the only way to God.
"...I am the way and the truth and the life. No one comes to the Father except through me." - John 14:6

This illustration shows that God has bridged the gap between Himself and man by sending Jesus Christ to die in our place as our substitute. Jesus defeated sin and death and rose from the grave. Yet, it isn't enough just to know these facts. To become a part of God's team, there must be...

Knowing a lot about a sport and "talking the game" doesn't make you a member of a team. The same is true in becoming a Christian. It takes more than just knowing about Jesus Christ; it requires a total commitment by faith in Him.

FAITH IS NOT:

Just knowing the facts.
"You believe that there is one God. Good! Even the demons believe that – and shudder."
- James 2:19

Just an emotional experience.
Raising your hand or repeating a prayer is not enough.

FAITH IS:

Repenting.
Turning to God from sin.
"Godly sorrow brings repentance that leads to salvation and leaves no regret..."
- 2 Corinthians 7:10a

Receiving Jesus Christ.
Trusting in Christ alone for salvation.
"Yet to all who received him, to those who believed in his name, he gave the right to become children of God..." - John 1:12

On which side of the illustration do you see yourself? Where would you like to be?

Jesus said, "I tell you the truth, whoever hears my word and believes him who sent me has eternal life and will not be condemned; he has crossed over from death to life." - John 5:24

To make sure we are making the right call, let's look at the...

Replay of God's Plan

- **REALIZE** God is holy and perfect; we are sinners and cannot save ourselves.
- **RECOGNIZE** who Jesus is and what He's done as our substitute.
- **REPENT** by turning to God from sin.
- **RECEIVE** Jesus Christ by faith as Savior and Lord.
- **RESPOND** to Jesus Christ in a life of obedience.

Jesus said, "...If anyone would come after me, he must deny himself and take up his cross daily and follow me." - Luke 9:23

Does God's plan make sense to you? Are you willing to repent and receive Jesus Christ? If so, express to God your need for Him. If you're not sure what to say, consider the "Suggested Prayer of Commitment" below. Remember that God is more concerned with your attitude than with the words you say.

SUGGESTED PRAYER OF COMMITMENT:

"Lord Jesus, I need you. I realize I'm a sinner, and I can't save myself. I need your mercy. I believe that you died on the cross for my sins and rose from the dead. I repent of my sins and put my faith in you as Savior and Lord. Take control of my life, and help me to follow you in obedience. In Jesus' name. Amen."

"...If you confess with your mouth, 'Jesus is Lord,' and believe in your heart that God raised him from the dead, you will be saved. ... for, 'Everyone who calls on the name of the Lord will be saved.' " - Romans 10:9,13

Once you have committed your life to Jesus Christ, it is important for you to...

Made in the USA
Monee, IL
20 February 2025

12310835R00024